KV-684-407

Contents

CHAPTER 1

What is this feeling?

THERE YOU ARE, savouring the last bits of the weekend. Then – bam! – an unfocused dread washes over you, and the pressures of the next week loom in your brain. You feel your chest tighten and your muscles tense. It might seem harder to breathe and much more difficult to think clearly. Even if you are holding it together on the outside, inside you are a hot mess. As the feeling grows, you may snap at the people around you who seem annoyingly unaware of the powerful panic sweeping over you.

DECODING
THE MIND

WHY WE WORRY

THE SCIENCE OF ANXIETY

Melissa Mayer

raintree

...pstone company — publishers for children

Raintree is an imprint of Capstone Global Library Limited, a company
incorporated in England and Wales having its registered office at 264
Banbury Road, Oxford, OX2 7DY – Registered company number: 6695582

www.raintree.co.uk
myorders@raintree.co.uk

Edited by Gina Kammer, Kellie M Hultgren
Designed by Brann Garvey
Original illustrations © Capstone Global Library Limited 2020
Picture research by Tracy Cummins
Production by Tori Abraham
Originated by Capstone Global Library Ltd
Printed and bound in India

978 1 4747 8922 6 (hardback)
978 1 4747 8929 5 (paperback)

British Library Cataloguing in Publication Data
A full catalogue record for this book is available from the British Library.

Acknowledgements
We would like to thank the following for permission to
photographs: Getty Images: Matt Winkelmeyer, 57; iStoc
ChrisRyan, 30; Shutterstock: Aaron Amat, 6, adike, 21, A
25, antoniodiaz, 4, Aurora72, 14, Billion Photos, 23, Blan
Studio, Cover, Designua, 20, Dmitry Pichugin, 28, 32, D
Featureflash Photo Agency, 55, fizkes, 51, iQoncept, 36,
Katrina Lee, 26 Top, kentoh, 13, KittyVector, 27, Kosko,
McElroy, 7, Monkey Business Images, 40, 44, MSSA, 29,
pathdoc, 5, Romanova Natali, 19, Salim Nasirov, 34, Tea
Ugis Riba, 8, Visual Generation, 35 Top, whitehoune, 49

Every effort has been made to contact copyright holders
reproduced in this book. Any omissions will be rectified
printings if notice is given to the publisher.

Men have had hysteria, too, especially during times of war.

Men have had hysteria, too, especially during times of war. Some men and boys who were expected to march off to battle suddenly found themselves unable to move their arms or legs. Military doctors reported this as hysterical paralysis, caused by intense anxiety and a desire to avoid shame, during World War I and more intensely during World War II.

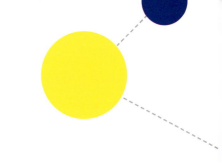

Meet the anxiety disorders

While anxiety is very common and usually tolerated by people who have it, too much anxiety can cause problems, and that is true for a lot of people. The National Institute of Mental Health says anxiety disorders are the most common of all mental health disorders, especially among young adults. The institute says almost one third of people aged between 13 and 18 years old have an anxiety disorder.

With those statistics, it makes sense to learn a bit about the types of anxiety disorders and how to know whether your anxiety is problematic. Lots of medical conditions cause symptoms of anxiety, but five basic mental health disorders have been defined.

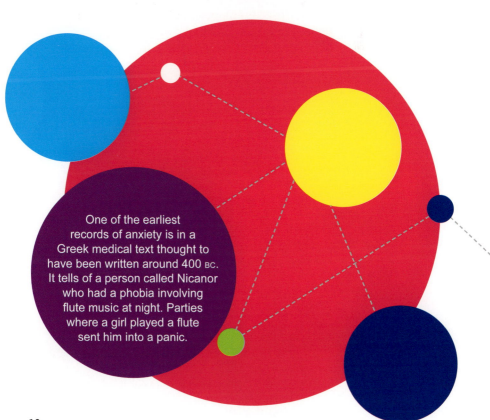

One of the earliest records of anxiety is in a Greek medical text thought to have been written around 400 BC. It tells of a person called Nicanor who had a phobia involving flute music at night. Parties where a girl played a flute sent him into a panic.

- **GENERALIZED ANXIETY DISORDER (GAD):** This is the most common type of anxiety. GAD is exactly what it sounds like. It is general excessive worry about a wide range of everyday topics, such as school or health. GAD may have physical symptoms such as fatigue, headaches, muscle pain and difficulty sleeping. Anxiety that is felt every day (or close to it) for at least six months might be GAD.

- **PANIC DISORDER:** This disorder brings – that's right – panic attacks. These are sudden rushes of fear or dread that feel very intense within minutes. A panic attack can cause physical symptoms such as sweating, a racing heart and hyperventilating – and it may feel like a medical emergency while it is happening (even though it isn't).

- **PHOBIAS:** Some people have intense, irrational fear attached to certain things or situations. Common phobias include fear of flying, heights, small spaces or certain animals. Social anxiety disorder, which causes an intense fear of feeling judged or embarrassed in front of people, is a phobia.

- **POST-TRAUMATIC STRESS DISORDER (PTSD):** This is a combination of symptoms that may appear after a shocking or life-threatening event, such as sexual violence, war or a car accident. One common symptom is reliving the trauma through flashbacks.

- **OBSESSIVE-COMPULSIVE DISORDER (OCD):** People with this condition have troubling thoughts and behaviours and do things repeatedly to try to calm themselves. For instance, if OCD causes people to worry about germs, they might wash their hands over and over again.

Anxiety has a price

The major problem with anxiety is that it can make your life harder. Anxiety can feel terrible, and it can also cause you to avoid things you might enjoy or that are important for you. For instance, if anxiety causes you to miss school, you may have problems with your teachers, your progress or even the law. Some young people who experience anxiety have a harder time later in life, such as during college or university or when they try to get a job.

Out-of-control anxiety might mean that you miss chances to be with friends or build solid relationships. This can lead to feeling alone, which can make anxiety even worse. Some people live in families that don't understand anxiety, which can make it harder to get support. If you are worried about your anxiety, you can talk to an adult you trust, such as a teacher, guidance counsellor, a nurse at school or your family doctor.

Medical experts believe that long-term anxiety – especially

"Anxiety and depression rates among teenagers are up 300 to 500 per cent compared with the rates of 50 years ago, according to researchers at San Diego State University, USA."

Michael Bradley, PhD, psychologist and author of *Crazy-Stressed*

untreated anxiety – can take a toll on physical health. People with medical conditions that affect the stomach, lungs or heart often have anxiety disorders too. Researchers have tried to understand whether untreated anxiety makes these conditions worse. Chronic stress can weaken the immune system, making it easier for you to become unwell. The physical symptoms that often come with anxiety, such as difficulty sleeping, exhaustion, headaches and muscle pain, can add up over time and cause problems and discomfort. Scientific findings show that stress can affect the bacteria in your gut. Imbalances in the types of bacteria in your digestive tract can cause stomach problems.

IT'S A BIRD!
IT'S A PLANE! IT'S . . .
SUPER ANXIETY!

The news isn't all doom and gloom. Some experts believe anxiety also has benefits that can make your life better. Anxiety might even mean you are more clever than your less-worried peers.

Scientists say people who are more anxious are also more alert, and they pay more attention to things. These characteristics may help people with anxiety predict outcomes better and perform better at work or school. It also makes them better at reading other people's emotions. This is probably because they scan faces and study expressions more intensely.

These abilities give anxious people what scientists call a selective advantage. The forces of evolution make sure that anxiety sticks around in human DNA. While too much anxiety is a problem, moderate anxiety – or the ability to manage a lot of anxiety with treatment – may point to higher intelligence and help you outperform those around you.

The word *anxiety* comes from the Latin word *angor*, which means *to constrict*, and is related to *angustus*, which means *narrow*. It shares an Indo-European root with the word *angst*.

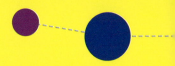

CHAPTER 2

A quick guide to neuroanatomy

I F YOU WANT TO UNDERSTAND (and handle) your anxiety, the first step is closer than you think. Look no further than the organ sitting between your ears. Your brain is where it all starts.

Meet your brain

You are minding your own business when you smell something familiar – vanilla. With that whiff, your interest is piqued, and your mood softens. For some reason your worries seem further away. Maybe you think about being 5 years old in your pyjamas, eating biscuits and watching cartoons. Or maybe you feel a wave of nausea. You think about the time you ate those biscuits until you were ill. It's as if you are right back there, feeling queasy and sick all over again.

It is easy to link smells with feelings because the areas in your brain that process your memories and emotions are connected to areas important for your sense of smell. Smells trigger memories and feelings so well that some shops actually pump certain nice smells into the air to make you more likely to buy things!

The parts of your brain responsible for storing and retrieving your memories are part of your limbic system. These areas also play a role in emotional regulation. This is your ability to feel all of your emotions in an appropriate and flexible way. Your limbic system allows you to have spontaneous feelings, yet also control your reactions. This skill is why most adults don't throw themselves on the floor, kicking and wailing, when they are upset. These areas of your brain also help you manage anxiety.

Some of the key players in the anxiety game are the amygdala, hypothalamus, hippocampus and prefrontal cortex. Don't worry, you don't need a degree in neuroscience to understand the parts these play inside your head.

Key players in the anxiety game

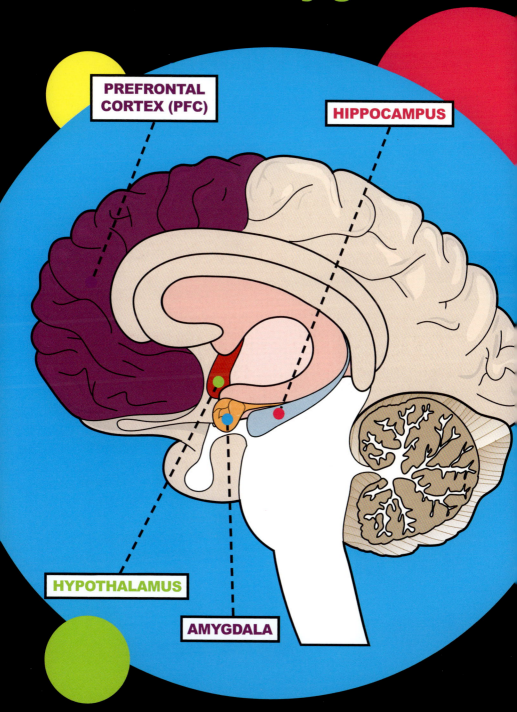

PREFRONTAL CORTEX (PFC)

HIPPOCAMPUS

HYPOTHALAMUS

AMYGDALA

Treatment for anxiety then was definitely different from today's. Doctors in ancient Egypt thought internal organs could move around randomly, on their own. To them, anxiety meant that a woman's uterus had moved to a place that was too high or too low. At the time, the obvious and not-at-all-strange medical response was to entice that pesky organ to move back to its proper spot. How to do this? With smells. By placing nice-smelling perfumes at one end of the patient's body and things that smelled awful at the other end, early doctors thought they could coax the organ to move towards the nice smell and away from the stinky one. That, they assumed, would put the organ back where it belonged.

Anxiety – called *hysteria* by Hippocrates in ancient Greece – has appeared a lot during human history. For instance, hundreds of women have been persecuted as witches through human history. Witch hunters believed that anxiety symptoms showed that a person had a pact with the devil. This was even more likely if the things the suspected witch worried about came true. Anxiety also seemed to be contagious. As accusations of witchcraft spread, hysteria could affect whole towns.

Or perhaps you do know what the week will bring and are sweating over the possibilities. What if you fail a test or do something embarrassing? Your mind conjures an array of possibilities (all negative) that you might encounter just around the corner. Some seem so likely to happen that you think them through over and over again until they seem to have worn a groove in your brain. You imagine conversations or watch a loop of worst-case scenarios in your mind's eye. You lie awake, paralyzed by dread, your mind racing. You wake up exhausted, tense and moody.

These are all signs of anxiety. And you aren't alone. Everyone experiences anxiety sometimes. Fortunately, scientists have learned a lot about how and why human brains are so prone to panic and worry. Digging into the history and science of anxiety may help you work with (and not fight) your (sometimes) anxious mind.

- **AMYGDALA:** Acts partly as your brain's alarm system. Its job is to take in data from your senses and press the alarm quickly if it suspects danger. You reach for something on a shelf and see a sudden spidery motion near your hand that makes you jump back before you even think. Pleased that you didn't grab a hairy spider? Thank your amygdala.

- **HYPOTHALAMUS:** Responds to the alarm set off by your amygdala by sending chemical messages through your body. These messages ensure that every part of you is ready to respond to the threat at the same time. This is why your body can pull back from the spider so quickly – because the parts of your body work as a team.

- **HIPPOCAMPUS:** Acts like a librarian who helps store your memories and pulls them out when they might benefit you. This area may not work properly under intense stress that causes a surge of hormones, so the memories you make during these times may be stored in a less organized and less accessible way. This is why you react strongly to some situations without knowing why. Your hippocampus also notes what has helped you with stress in the past so you can respond better when similar stress appears in the future.

- **PREFRONTAL CORTEX (PFC):** Your brain's command centre. Your PFC receives sensory data more slowly than your amygdala. It uses your memories and extra data to consider all your responses. When your amygdala sounds the alarm about that spider, making you jump, your PFC points out that the window is open and blowing debris onto the shelf in a spooky way. Your PFC tells you the threat is not real. You don't have to burn your house down to escape the evil spider after all. Your PFC is part of your cerebral cortex, which is the big mass of wrinkly tissue you probably picture when you hear the word *brain*.

Your brain talks to itself

To provoke your anxiety (and to stop it) all of these areas of your brain need to be on the same page. Human emergency response people, such as firefighters or paramedics, use radio transmitters so they can pass messages back and forth from the scene. Your brain does something very similar. It uses chemicals called *neurotransmitters* that carry messages from nerve cell to nerve cell. This allows the regions of your brain to work together. Some well-known neurotransmitters are adrenaline, dopamine, oxytocin and serotonin.

Common neurotransmitters and possible results

ADRENALINE	EMERGENCY RESPONSE
DOPAMINE	REWARD SEEKING
OXYTOCIN	LOVE AND BONDING
SEROTONIN	HAPPINESS

Nerve cells (neurons) in your brain look a bit like fireworks with tails. Each neuron has a cell body surrounded by dendrites, which look like the branches of a tree reaching out. It also has a long tail called an *axon* with branches at its tip. Neurons don't touch each other, so in order to send messages, they launch neurotransmitters out of the axon tail into the empty space between neurons. These spaces are called *synapses*. Other neurons use their branchy dendrites to catch these chemical messages, which fit into them like a key into a lock. If enough chemical signals are received, a neuron fires, which is like a surge of electricity that runs down the length of the neuron. This causes the neuron to release a chemical message through its axon ending, passing the signal to one of its neighbouring nerve cells.

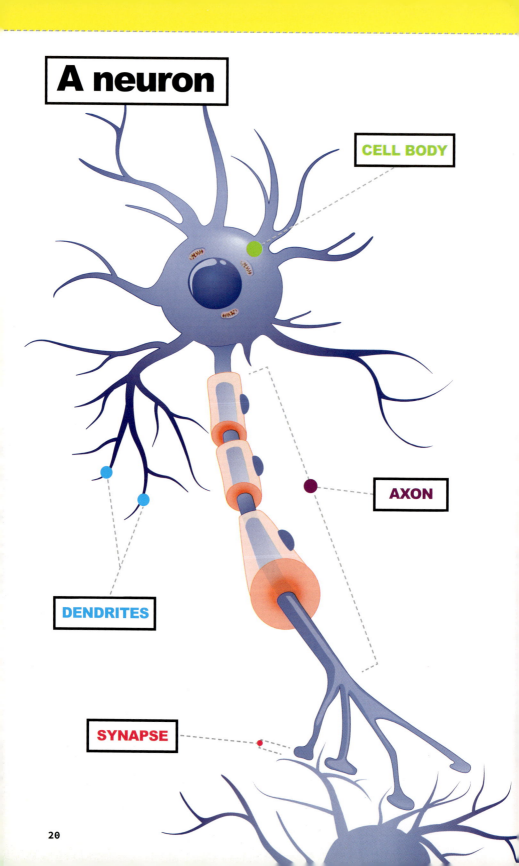

A neuron

CELL BODY

AXON

DENDRITES

SYNAPSE

When your neurons pass messages, the connections between them may become stronger. This is called *firing together*. When neurons fire together, the path the message takes from one nerve cell to the next becomes easier. This means the messages can travel faster and more reliably. The first few times you wrote your name, it probably seemed really hard. Even making one letter was hard work. Now you write your name on autopilot. That's because when neurons fire together again and again, it becomes easier over time to form the same thought or to perform the same task.

The way your neurons fire together also helps your brain make sense of the world. Neurons that fire together form circuits a bit like electrical circuits in your home. The circuits become associations in your mind. This is why you might link the smell of a dental office with the idea of pain or fun, depending on your experience at the dentist. It is also why you can see a dog and feel love or joy while someone else might feel fear. Scientists say: "Neurons that fire together wire together".

The most likely culprits

The ways your amygdala and prefrontal cortex work together are neuroscientist-level complex. Some brain experts use a simpler tool to help people understand and manage anxiety. They divide anxiety into two types, based on the brain area most strongly linked to it: the cerebral cortex pathway and the amygdala pathway.

The cerebral cortex is the largest part of your brain. The wrinkly tissue that zombies enjoy eating? That's your cortex. Your brain has two sides (left and right) and your cortex is further divided into many areas with various functions. The cortex does the most complex thinking, and the frontal lobe handles what scientists call *executive functions*. These are things like planning, paying attention and keeping track of what you are doing. To do these things, you need to be able to make predictions and imagine consequences. These very skills can also produce the key feature of the cortex type of anxiety: worry. If the anxiety you feel includes worry and imagining worst-case scenarios, it probably comes from your cerebral cortex.

You have an amygdala structure on each side of your brain. Each one is about 1.5 cm in size and shaped like an almond. Your amygdala scans for danger and gives you emotional reactions to things. The amygdala pathway can be summed up in one word: quick. Your brain takes in data using your senses and sends that information in two directions – to the cortex for processing and to the amygdala for rapid response. Your amygdala either sends out an alarm or does nothing before your cortex even gets the data. If the anxiety you feel is sudden panic or dread, it probably comes from your amygdala.

"Feelings like disappointment, embarrassment, irritation, resentment, anger, jealousy and fear, instead of being bad news, are actually very clear moments that teach us where it is that we're holding back. They teach us to perk up and lean in when we feel we'd rather collapse and back away. They're like messengers that show us . . . exactly where we're stuck. This very moment is the perfect teacher and, luckily for us, it's with us wherever we are."

Pema Chödrön,
Buddhist nun, teacher, and author of *When Things Fall Apart*

EVEN YOUR GENES ARE ANXIOUS

If you have a lot of anxiety, you probably don't have to look far to find someone else who does. Anxiety disorders run in families. In fact, having a close family member with an anxiety disorder makes it more likely that you will develop one. Some families don't talk openly about mental health, and some people don't know their biological relatives, but if you have this information it might help you know whether anxiety runs in your family.

Genetics is very complicated. It is impossible to work out how much of your anxiety comes from your genes and how much is because of your environment. For example, living with an anxious parent might teach you anxious behaviours, even if it wasn't encoded in your DNA.

In recent years, scientists have discovered that your experiences can leave marks on your DNA. The marks can change the way your genes produce effects in you, and the changes may even be passed on to your children. For instance, those marks on the genes of the children of Holocaust survivors may make them more likely to develop a stress disorder even though they did not live through the trauma. A study found that mice with comfortable lives – mice that had lots of food and toys – gave birth to more intelligent baby mice.

Scientists think bad experiences can mark your DNA, but so can healthy choices, such as eating nutritious foods, exercising and getting enough good sleep. It's as though the good choices could buffer any bad things that come your way. You can't choose your genes, but all the healthy things you do will add up.

CHAPTER 3

Fight or flight (or freeze):
the value of fear

SOMEONE YOU DON'T KNOW well comes up to you at school. She is clearly angry, and before you know it, she is in your face. She is so close that you can smell her lunch on her breath. You feel a burst of rage, and, without thinking, you push her as hard as you can out of your personal space.

Or… you are taking out the rubbish one evening when you hear twigs snapping behind you. It's too dark to see, but you feel prickling on the back of your neck. You sense that someone – or something – is out there with you. You drop the rubbish and run as fast as your legs will carry you back into your well-lit home.

Or… something jolts you out of a deep sleep. Your room is dark, with only a strip of light coming in under your bedroom door. The house is silent. Suddenly you hear the sound of footsteps and see a shadow darken the light below your door. You can't move. You try to open your mouth to scream, but nothing comes out. You lie completely still and silent in your bed, staring at the door as you see the door handle begin to turn.

You have just experienced a stress response, also called a *fight-or-flight response*. You took in data using your five senses, and your amygdala set off the alarm: you are in danger! Before your cortex even gets the sensory data, and well before you can form a thought, your amygdala has already alerted your hypothalamus, and your stress response is underway.

Your hypothalamus gets the signal and sends out chemical messages. Your neurons receive the messages from their neighbours and release others. The messaging triggers your adrenal glands, which begin dumping adrenaline into your bloodstream. As this message reaches your organs, changes happen rapidly. Your heart beats faster, sending more blood to your muscles for energy and oxygen. You breathe faster and more deeply so you can pull in more oxygen with every breath. All that oxygen hits your brain, making you more alert and sharpening your senses. Your body begins to load stored sugar and fat into your blood so that you have as much energy as possible. At the same time, your body puts other systems (like digestion) on hold to free up energy.

Your amygdala screams, "This is not a drill! The emergency is here! All hands on deck!" You are a taut elastic band of potential energy, ready to snap into action. You have three options: fight the threat, run fast and far or freeze.

Fight or flight is a response to stress.

FLIGHT

FREEZE

FIGHT

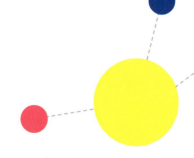

Your prehistoric ancestors

Fight-or-flight is an ideal system when you face danger. It was vitally important during prehistoric times, when the threats your ancestors faced were clear (and big and possibly snarling). Contrary to cartoons, early humans were not fierce hunters. In fact, your earliest ancestors were more likely to be the prey than the predator. They probably spent most of their time gathering plants, scavenging carcasses for leftovers and hiding from animals that saw them as a pleasantly hairless dessert.

Predators lurked everywhere: sabre-toothed cats, cave bears and snakes, to name a few. Add to that the possibility of natural accidents, being trampled by giant animals and the many risks of living in a world without advanced technology or medical knowledge. There were terrors galore.

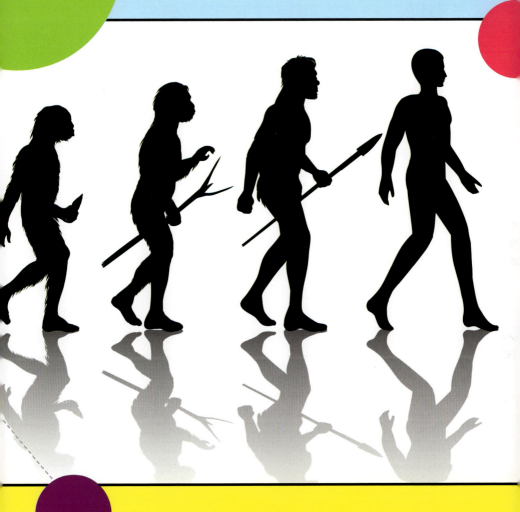

For pre-historic humans, stepping outside meant facing a world filled with threats to survival. To stay alive long enough to reproduce and pass on genes (so you could eventually be born), women needed a method to alert them to threats. In addition to this, they had to be able to spring into action before they could even consider their options. Early humans without strong stress responses would not have made it back to the cave.

Primitive responses and modern danger

Of course, the stress you face today is very different from the stress early humans faced . . . or is it? It seems reasonable that the instincts that helped cave people leap away from a herd of stampeding mammoths also aid modern humans facing a pair of oncoming headlights.

On the other hand, modern humans are not usually focused on basic survival. Thanks to technology, you probably don't spend all your time looking for your next roadkill meal (yum, still warm!) or hiding from animals that want to eat you. Even considering school and homework, you probably have time for hobbies, entertainment, and even (gasp) boredom – a possibility that might seem shocking and appalling to prehistoric humans.

These changes mean that your inherited stress response may not be very helpful with modern stress. If you are like most tweens or teens, your anxiety may centre on academic stress, puberty, friendships and planning for your future. While those things are no doubt stressful, they are unlikely to kill you in the next five minutes. Those chemical messages pumping through your brain and in your bloodstream, thanks to your amygdala's alarm, can harm your body when it happens often.

"Giftedness and ability can be sharpened by manageable levels of anxiety."

Gail Saltz, psychiatrist, clinical associate professor of psychiatry and author of *The Power of Different: The Link Between Disorder and Genius*

Your prehistoric stress response also produces what experts call *attentional bias to threat*, especially among people who tend to be anxious. If your amygdala sets off the "danger" alarm often, the lesson the brain takes is that you live in a very dangerous place. This belief can make you focus on possible threats. To study this, scientists show people photos of neutral faces and angry faces. People with anxiety tend to look at the angry face first and for a longer time.

The downside is that focusing on danger can give you tunnel vision. This means the safe or good things are often blocked from your view, and all you see are the dangerous or bad things. Did you know that you are living in the safest time in human history? According to experts, the big picture in terms of human history is a trend towards a safer, more just world. To view this data yourself, check out the grant-funded website: Our World in Data.

TRUSTING YOUR GUT

You meet someone new, and she seems perfectly nice. She says and does all the right things. She is likeable. Maybe you even have friends in common who say she is great. Despite all of this, a voice inside you screams that something is off. It isn't just that you don't like her; it's that something feels *wrong*. Are you right to trust your feeling about this person – or not?

You might call this voice your intuition or your gut. A consultant on violent behaviour, Gavin de Becker, calls it your gift. According to de Becker, being able to tell random fear from actual fear – the voice telling you about a real threat – is the ultimate present passed down to you from your ancestors. If you can train yourself to identify fear that comes from your gut and to know when to listen to it, no matter what anyone else says, you are using your natural instincts to keep you safe.

Sometimes people downplay this voice as "just a feeling", but you now know that many of the feelings you have, including anxiety, are the result of your brain gathering sensory data. A gut feeling is not something magical that just happens. It is your brain responding to something you notice that seems wrong or dangerous – even if you can't say exactly why.

CHAPTER 4

Handling anxiety like a boss

So YOU UNDERSTAND what your anxiety is and where it comes from, but what can you *do* about it? Quite a lot, actually. There are lots of tools you can use to deal with anxiety – and they work even better if you can find out what kind of anxiety you usually have.

Amygdala or cortex?

If your brain came with an instruction manual it might sort anxiety into two categories, depending on its pathway. You have already met your amygdala and cortex, and you know that these areas serve very different purposes. Your amygdala scans for threats and sets off an alarm that triggers fight-or-flight. Your cortex receives the same sensory data more slowly and uses skills like predicting outcomes and imagining consequences to process it.

In other words, amygdala-based anxiety is quick and panicky while cortex-based anxiety features worry and negative thoughts.

Amygdala or cortex anxiety?

AMYGDALA	CORTEX
You often feel as if you can't control your emotions.	You rehearse or imagine what will go wrong and how you will respond.
You suddenly feel anxious or panicky. Sometimes you are calm one moment and panicked the next.	You think about the past and how you might have done things differently.
Some places or things make you very uncomfortable, but you can't explain why.	You like to have responses ready for all possible problems. You think about problems from every angle.
You can't always work out what is making you feel panicky.	You sometimes feel like you can't escape negative thoughts.
You suddenly feel physical symptoms: a pounding or racing heart, sweating or difficulty breathing.	You sometimes feel stuck thinking about all the ways to solve a real or imaginary problem.
Sometimes you overreact. You might feel as if you will explode or snap.	You pay extra attention to others' tone and body language.
Sometimes it starts to feel as though things aren't real, or your mind goes blank.	You imagine bad things that could happen – being ill, being embarrassed, worst-case scenarios.

Tame your amygdala

There are clear signs that your amygdala has hit the alarm button and is now running the show. These include sweating, rapid breathing, tense muscles, a pounding heart, trouble focusing, trembling and feeling an urge to fight, run away or freeze. During a panic attack, you might also feel a sense of dread or terror or that you are outside of reality. You may wonder whether you are crazy or even dying.

Trying to reason with yourself or use rational thinking to climb out of a panic attack is pointless. It just won't work. Instead you need tools that show your amygdala that the danger has passed. These are deep breathing, exercise and muscle relaxation.

DEEP BREATHING

DEEP BREATHING CALMS YOU.
Panic can make you breathe too quickly and take in too little oxygen. This is why you sometimes feel dizzy or tingly. Intentional deep breathing fixes these symptoms and tells your stress response to relax.

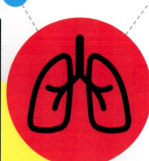

HOW TO BELLY BREATHE

Place one hand on your chest and one on your stomach near your belly button. Let out an annoyed sigh. (You can even say UGH.) With your mouth closed, slowly draw in air through your nose in a way that makes your stomach expand while your chest remains mostly still. Pause for a few seconds then use your stomach muscles to slowly push the air out of your mouth. Repeat.

EXERCISE

EXERCISE SHORTENS A PANIC ATTACK. During a stress response, your body moves stored energy into your blood so you are ready to outrun a tiger or lift a car off a baby. If you can burn some of that energy, your amygdala will believe it has done its job. Pace. Run in circles. Do some jumping jacks. Burn that energy.

MUSCLE RELAXATION

MUSCLE RELAXATION HELPS AVOID OR SHORTEN PANIC ATTACKS. When your amygdala is in charge, your muscles are tight. You are a tensed coil ready to spring into action. Relaxing your muscles is a physical way to tell your amygdala that the threat is over.

HOW TO RELAX YOUR MUSCLES

Begin with an easy-to-isolate muscle group like your hands. Clench your fists as tightly as you can. Feel all the muscles in your hands and fingers and make them as tense as possible. Now release those muscles. Try to let your hands and fingers relax as much as they can. Do this for the other muscles in your body.

Your stress response relies on feedback loops. This means that your body relies on the data inside it to either keep the stress response going or bring it to an end. Feedback loops also tell your amygdala how well the panic worked to protect you from the sabre-toothed cat. When your body has learnt a pattern, it can respond even faster in the future.

For this reason, it is important to ignore your urge to flee or freeze if you can. Fleeing might feel better now, but it will make you more likely to panic again in the future – because your amygdala will think that this strategy worked. Giving in to the urge to freeze may cause you to avoid things. This can isolate you from others and make your anxiety worse over time. Choosing an active coping strategy instead of freezing reroutes your anxiety away from the freeze response.

"It's common to have erroneous, unrealistic or illogical thoughts or to experience emotions that don't make much sense. In reality, you need not take every thought or emotion you have seriously. You can allow many thoughts and emotions to simply pass without undue attention or analysis."

Catherine Pittman, clinical psychologist, chair of the Department of Psychology at St. Mary's College, Notre Dame, Indiana, USA, and co-author of *Rewire Your Anxious Brain*

Some long-term activities can help too. These include good habits like exercising, getting enough sleep and practising relaxation techniques such as meditation. It might also help to identify your triggers – the sensations, objects or events that set off your anxiety. Learning about your triggers and trying to calm them are great things to tackle with a therapist or counsellor.

Soothe your cortex

Unlike your amygdala, your cortex is a deep thinker. It responds well to cognitive approaches and reasoning. A therapist can even help you restructure your thinking. One common type of talk therapy, cognitive behavioural therapy, is designed just for this purpose. Your cortex also responds well to self-help tools and mental tricks.

The most important thing to remember when it comes to your cortex is this: don't believe everything your brain tells you. An idea can pop into your head without being true. Here are simple things to practise to reduce cortex-type anxiety:

- **Use thought stopping to halt negative thinking.** If you find yourself being buried by a mountain of worry and other negative thoughts, tell yourself: STOP! Then intentionally replace your thought. You can rephrase the negative thought to make it something positive. Or you can replace it with a simple affirmation. For example, you keep thinking about all the terrible things that could ruin a class presentation. When you start to think about forgetting everything and just standing there humiliated in front of everyone, tell yourself: STOP! Then replace that thought: *I won't forget what to say because I have practised and have note cards. I've got this!*

- **Switch the anxiety channel.** If you find yourself imagining worst-case scenarios or obsessing about what might happen, pretend your brain is a music-streaming service and you can skip to another song or channel. You can even tell your brain that's what you are doing. "No, I'm not going to listen to this now. I'm changing the song." Then focus on something else. You may need to do this a few times in a row at first, but with practice it will become easier.

POWERFUL WORDS FOR POWERFUL WORRY

Here are some tried-and-tested affirmations for thought stopping.
This too shall pass.
Lots of people feel this way.
Feel the fear and do it anyway.
I am in control of my thoughts and my life.
I love myself unconditionally.
I've got this.
I'm not thinking about this now.

- **Set a date with anxiety.** Sometimes it just feels impossible to stop negative thoughts. Try picking a certain time to worry. Put it in your phone or write it down: Worry Date – 5 pm, Friday. Every time you start to worry, remind yourself. "Ah, this isn't the Worry Date. I'll put it to one side and make sure I worry about it on Friday." It sounds silly, but for your rational cortex, it makes sense.

- **Play more.** Did you know that one of the most powerful tools you have is your ability to have fun? Play is one way humans make sense of the world, learn things and release stress. If you are feeling anxious, think of something fun or funny and dive into it (even if you don't feel like doing it).

"If the rise in anxiety and depression [is] linked to a decline in sense of personal control, then play would seem to be the perfect remedy. A fundamental characteristic of play . . . is that it is directed and controlled by the players themselves."

Peter Gray, PhD, research professor and author of *Psychology* and *Free to Learn*

MINDFULNESS TRAINING

Your mind probably likes to run away to other places and times. It enjoys obsessing about things from the past or freaking out about the future. *Mindfulness* means keeping your mind in the present moment.

One way to root yourself in the present is to use your senses like reference points. Notice the sounds, smells, tastes, sights and sensations you are experiencing right now. Carefully focus on the small details you usually ignore.

For example, make yourself a snack. Turn off everything except your focus on that snack and the act of eating it. Notice how it looks and smells. How does it feel in your hand and in your mouth? Do you taste it in all the parts of your mouth? This narrowed focus is mindfulness.

You can be mindful with your anxiety too. This means noticing all the things happening in your mind and your body without judging or trying to stop them. Simply notice how anxiety feels to you and your body.

CHAPTER 5

When to worry about worry

A T SOME POINT YOU MIGHT wonder whether you should seek help for your anxiety. You know why anxiety exists and you appreciate the way it urges you to stay safe and do your best. You understand the major players in the stress response and how to steer your brain away from panic attacks and worry. But how do you know when your anxiety is going too far?

The Anxiety and Depression Association has an answer for you. Your anxiety might become a problem if you have these red flags:

- **It develops often and lasts a long time**. Have you felt anxious almost every day for the last six months?

- **It doesn't make sense**. Do you panic or worry about things that are unlikely to happen or that would seem unreasonable to other people?

- **It feels as though you can't control it**. Do you feel overwhelmed or as if you can't escape your anxiety?

- **It messes up your life**. Does your anxiety stop you from doing things you want to do, such as going to school, seeing your friends and having hobbies?

Other red flags are sometimes called *maladaptive behaviours*. These are harmful things some people do to try to deal with anxiety. Some aren't too bad. For instance, you might bite your fingernails. This may soothe your anxiety in the moment, but it can leave your fingers sore and invite infection. There are also more serious maladaptive behaviours, and these are red flags that indicate you should reach out for help. These include:

- **Disordered eating or exercising**, which can happen if you closely control how much you eat or exercise. You might not be eating enough, exercising too much or having times when you eat too much or throw up after eating.

- **Self-harm**, which is causing pain or damage to your body by cutting, burning or scratching your skin to release emotional pain or anxiety.

- **Substance abuse**, which is using drugs or alcohol to numb your anxiety.

If you notice any red flags in your experience of anxiety, it is important to ask for help. Having anxiety that has become a problem does not mean you are ill or broken or mad. Needing support for anxiety is common. You deserve to feel in charge of your life and your anxiety.

Anxiety disorders

You briefly met the most common anxiety disorders in Chapter 1. Now check out some of their signs. Everyone will probably relate to some of these sometimes – and that doesn't mean you have an anxiety disorder. However, if any of these descriptions raise red flags to you, talk to an adult you trust. Only a mental health professional can properly diagnose and treat an anxiety disorder.

Some signs of anxiety disorders

PEOPLE WITH GENERALIZED ANXIETY DISORDER (GAD):	• Have worry that is out of sync with reality. They may overthink and make plans for worst-case situations. • May believe that neutral things are dangerous. • Find uncertainty or making decisions difficult. • May always feel on edge or as if they can't relax. • Have trouble concentrating or feel that their mind goes blank. • Sometimes have trouble sleeping, resulting in exhaustion and irritability. • May feel tense and achy or trembly. • Sometimes have symptoms like sweating or digestive problems.
PEOPLE WITH A PANIC DISORDER:	• Have panic attacks, which are sudden and intense periods of fear without a reason. • Sometimes think they are dying or going crazy during a panic attack. • Sometimes feel extreme fear that they will have a panic attack. • Have panic attacks that include feeling out of control, worrying about death, a pounding heart, chills or hot flushes, trouble breathing, sweating, nausea, pain in the chest, head or stomach, dizziness and feeling disconnected.

PEOPLE WITH PHOBIAS:	• Have an intense, irrational fear of a certain object or situation. Some people have more than one phobia. • Might have common phobias, such as fear of flying, heights, storms, small spaces, blood or animals. • May feel panic when they are near the thing they fear. • Might try to avoid those things, even if it damages their life. • May have physical reactions like sweating or trouble breathing. • Sometimes know that their panic is irrational, but they can't stop it.
PEOPLE WITH POST-TRAUMATIC STRESS DISORDER (PTSD):	• Experienced something life-threatening or terrifying. Symptoms may show up straight away or years later. • Often have intrusive thoughts, including flashbacks, nightmares or memories of what happened. • May try to avoid things that remind them of what happened. They might not want to talk or think about it. • Sometimes feel bad about themselves and the future. They may disconnect from people or activities they once loved. • May have memory problems or feel numb. • May be irritable or easy to startle. • May feel unable to let down their guard and so have trouble sleeping or concentrating. • Sometimes feel guilty or ashamed.
PEOPLE WITH OBSESSIVE-COMPULSIVE DISORDER (OCD):	• Have irrational thoughts they can't shake off. They may repeatedly do certain things to try to stop the thoughts. For example, some people think about germs and then wash things over and over again. • May have intrusive thoughts about hurting themselves or other people.

How to get help

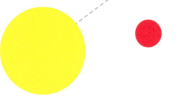

If you think your anxiety might be a problem, or if you suspect you have an anxiety disorder, it is important that you seek help. You might start by talking to your school counsellor or nurse. Anxiety and anxiety disorders are treatable. This means you can feel better! The best thing you can do is get help from someone trained to treat anxiety.

Mental health professionals may be therapists, clinical social workers, counsellors, psychologists or psychiatrists. They will have special training to diagnose and treat mental health problems. They should be licensed by the government. Choosing a licensed professional means you can trust that they will follow the rules and use therapy methods that are backed up by science. Check a professional database, such as the directory on the Mind UK website: www.mind.org.uk

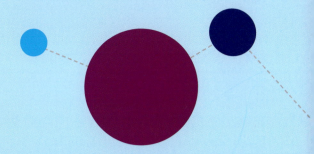

Many therapists list the types of problems they usually treat, so you can look for someone who is an expert in anxiety. If you know that something other than anxiety might come up during your therapy (for example, LGBTQ identity or substance abuse) it is a good idea to make sure these things are on the therapist's list too. As it is likely you will be sharing a lot with your therapist, it is important that you like the therapist and that he or she shares your values.

If you or your parents or guardians are unsure about where to start, here are some places where you can ask for a referral:

- Your school nurse

- Your GP

- A clinic or hospital

Reaching out for support isn't always easy, and some people face extra barriers. For instance, some people have cultural beliefs about mental health that make it harder for them to seek support. People of colour have the same rates of mental health disorders as their white peers, but they are much less likely to seek treatment. US organizations such as the Boris Lawrence Henson Foundation and the Steve Fund hope to change this. They are working to end stigmas attached to mental illness and health care among people of colour, and they are trying to increase cultural awareness and sensitivity among therapists.

Some people worry that money is a barrier to therapy. Free or low-cost options include finding a counsellor who uses

Only about 20 per cent of people between 13 and 18 years of age with a diagnosable anxiety disorder receive treatment.

a sliding scale or a donation-based support group run by professional therapists at a local community centre. Talk to your doctor, as you may well qualify for free NHS therapy and support.

Privacy concerns may also make it hard for people under the age of 18 to get help. Young people who are LGBTQ and live with unsupportive families may worry about being outed by a therapist or undergoing therapy that doesn't affirm their identities. Teenagers who use drugs or alcohol may be afraid of being punished or worry about disappointing people they love.

The recent uptake in hate crimes may trigger anxiety, especially for people who live in the affected communities. It may be hard to balance wanting to hear the news about hate crimes and needing to take care of yourself.

Whatever you situation, you don't need to face anxiety alone. The Crisis Text Line is open 24-hours a day – just text SHOUT to 85258.

If you suspect your anxiety is linked to a painful experience, look for a therapist with training in trauma-informed care. This type of treatment focuses on trust and support to help you feel safe and in control.

WHAT HAPPENS IN THERAPY?

Visiting a therapist can feel strange, especially if you are private about your feelings. Sometimes people worry that seeing a therapist means they are going crazy. This is not true! Your therapist can help you solve problems and make sure that the way you handle anxiety is healthy.

The most important thing to know about therapy is that you have the right to confidentiality. The things you tell a therapist or counsellor should be kept private. However, it is important to ask your therapist what, if anything, he or she would need to tell your parents. This is because the law is unclear when it comes to minors, and you should know what to expect before you begin therapy.

At your first therapy appointment, you will learn about your therapist's practice and background. This includes the types of treatment usually used and the therapist's special training. Some therapists give homework between sessions (usually practising skills you will learn in your session). The first meeting is a chance for you to ask questions and to make sure this therapist is a good fit for you. Think of it like an interview – and you are the one who can ask the questions!

When you begin seeing your therapist, either you or the therapist can suggest something to talk about. The therapist will probably take notes. This gives the therapist a way to review your progress before each visit. Some people attend therapy only a few times. Other people visit a therapist once or twice a week for years. Some people go to therapy alone. Others go with another person (such as a parent or partner). Some therapists offer group therapy, so several people with similar concerns can work together with the therapist and help each other.

CHAPTER 6

You are resilient

THERE IS GOOD NEWS: if you are anxious, you can feel better. You have the tools to manage your panic and worry, and your brain is set up to work with you. When it comes to anxiety, your brain is not an evil villain throwing panic in your path. Your brain is YOU, the hero of the story – and it has the power to morph to make you even stronger.

Your plastic brain . . . eats itself

You might imagine that Baby You came into the world with your brain built and ready to go and that your nerve cells don't change much after birth, but this isn't true. Your brain changes all the time. Scientists call this neuroplasticity. The brain is not firm and unyielding like metal. Instead, it's flexible – like plastic. While you can't literally reach inside your head and mould it like a giant chunk of clay, you can use your brain's adaptable nature to your benefit.

One thing that does change in your brain is the number of neurons. Adults add about 700 new neurons every single day (and necessarily lose many more). This takes place mainly in the hippocampus and smell centres. The new brain cells are important for learning, memory and emotional regulation – including dealing with anxiety.

Your synapses also change a lot over time. When you were 2 years old, you had about 15,000 synapses per neuron. That is, each brain cell had 15,000 places to make connections with its neighbours. Between toddlerhood and your early 20s, about half of those synapses go away through a process called *synaptic pruning*. Pruning makes it sound as if your brain is a tree someone is snipping into shape – and that isn't too far from the truth, although the actual truth is even stranger.

Inside your brain, microglial cells remove damage or infection using a process called *phagocytosis*, which means "to devour". These cells basically travel through your brain and eat things that can cause problems. Scientists recently discovered that this includes nibbling around your synapses – AKA synaptic pruning.

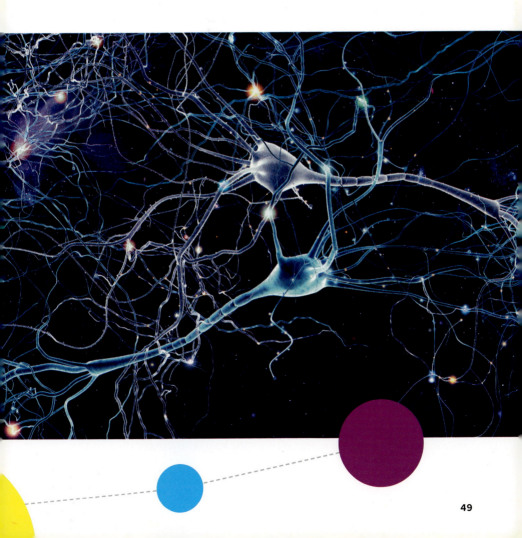

Resilience?
Not a problem!

The idea that a person's hippocampus pumps out new brain cells and the Pac-Man-like microglia eat your brain into shape is interesting, but how does it help you adapt? Brain plasticity is closely related to resilience. This is your ability to adapt to stresses and bounce back. Your plastic brain changes as part of its normal development, but it also changes when things get tough.

Stress and trauma can even shrink parts of your brain. This can happen to your hippocampus, prefrontal cortex and the branchy arms of your neurons. But wait: there's good news. Positive experiences can change the brain in the opposite way, enlarging the areas that stress shrinks. These include things like exercise, learning new things, social support and mindfulness exercises. Some scientists say these behaviours open "windows of plasticity", giving your brain the chance to bounce back from stress – and making you more resilient in the face of adversity.

Your plastic brain changes as part of its normal development...

Think back over human history. Humans have gone from being a cave bear's favourite meal to being tech-savvy makers and explorers travelling the oceans, space, the insides of atomic particles and even the human mind. Those very human impulses to survive and thrive? That is your legacy. That incredible resilience is the spark that your greatest grandmother, busy hiding from sabre-toothed cats and runaway mammoths, carried in her DNA. That same spark passed to people from every era of human history until it reached you. And now you carry it, buried in your genetic code, kept alive in every single cell in your body.

Whatever your worries may be – problems at school, money problems in your family, insecurities about who you are and what your future will look like, even anxieties about the future of the planet – you have the resources inside yourself to face these problems and more. These are your snarling tigers and stampeding mammoths. You come from a long line of people who used that spark of resilience to survive and make the world better, just as you will now.

Is it strange to think back to long-dead humans passing on their strength to you? Maybe. But taking a long, positive view of who you are and the role you play in the history of human awesomeness is also a great way to cultivate your resilience. Putting your own story into context might just help to make you stronger.

. . . you have the resources inside yourself to face these problems and more.

Make connections

Take decisive actions

Avoid seeing crises as insurmountable problems

Look for opportunities for self-discovery

Maintain a hopeful outlook

Keep things in perspective

Move towards your goals

Accept that change is a part of living

Ways to build resilience

Nurture a positive view of yourself

Take care of yourself

You need a crew – and the world needs you

Your ancestors were not solitary creatures, wandering around alone. Humans don't hatch their young and leave them to fend for themselves like tiny adults, as some animals do. Early humans relied on each other to combine resources and abilities because there is strength in numbers. Feeling like part of a supportive community is a key to resilience. But you don't need a perfect family or friendship group. In fact, having just one person who loves you can make a difference. Even if that person isn't with you right now, your built-in resilience is there for you – and it can help you reach out and find others who appreciate you.

Some people fit easily into their families and communities and build connections that last forever. Other people have chosen families or collections of people who understand them and give them support. While there is value in being with people in real life, online connections can be just as real as "real life" friendships. Don't discount your people, no matter where you find them.

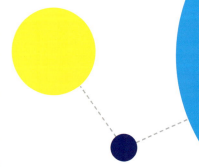

"What are we supposed to do with the evidence that shows that the very things than can cause our lives to be difficult (our inability to relate easily to others, or learning differences or mood disorders, for example) often come with unique skills and aptitudes (artistic abilities, creativity, a knack for remembering numbers or names or an ability to visualize data in a unique way)? And is it possible that if we focused not on the diagnoses or labels but on all the potential – the spark – that comes with our brain differences, we could access our unique abilities to contribute to our families, communities and the world in a new way?"

Gail Saltz, psychoanalyst, clinical associate professor of psychiatry and author of *The Power of Different: The Link Between Disorder and Genius*

COMMUNITY HEROES JUST LIKE YOU: TARAJI HENSON

Racial prejudice affects many communities and causes stress for the people in them. This can make anxiety worse. Because some prejudice is embedded in the way basic institutions work in society, avoiding it can seem impossible.

In the United States, Brown University offers students ways to cope with race-related stress. It recommends building a solid sense of your cultural identity and a support network of people who share your experience. Another tool is to use that strong sense of self to take social action in the world around you.

Actor Taraji Henson did just that in 2018 when she launched the Boris Lawrence Henson Foundation. The organization's aim is to find out why African Americans are less likely than white people to seek mental health care. Part of its strategy is to partner with schools to ensure mental health support is much more accessible.

Taraji Henson is a hero because she saw a need in her community and she stepped up to meet it.

Helping other people lowers your stress and may even be good for your physical wellbeing.

COMMUNITY HEROES JUST LIKE YOU: RUBY NOBOA

According to the National Alliance on Mental Illness (NAMI), people who identify as LGBTQ are about three times more likely to have anxiety as their cisgender, straight peers. If people grew up in a world with a narrow view of what is normal, it would be easy to feel abnormal. Experiences of injustice or rejection can add up over time. Experts call this *minority stress.*

Everyone needs a network of support and a sense of community, and this is especially true for people who feel minority stress. This is why some teenagerss form support groups in their schools or community such as gay-straight alliances (GSAs). These groups offer LGBTQ students a place to find support with each other and with peers who are allies.

GLSEN is a national organization in the United States that works to create safe schools for all students. Every year, it honours people who are working towards that goal. The 2018 GLSEN student advocate of the year, Ruby Noboa, helped form a GSA support group at her school and now speaks out on social justice issues. For her end-of-year project, Noboa planned to strengthen support resources in her community by opening an LGBTQ youth centre in the Bronx, New York, USA.

Ruby Noboa is a hero because she helps other people feel safe. Stepping into a leadership role in your community is a great way to channel your resilience in a way that helps the people around you who need it most – and also yourself!

Sometimes it's easy to overlook one of the simplest ways to build community and combat anxiety: volunteering. Experts call this *prosocial behaviour* – things you choose to do that help other people. Helping other people lowers your stress and may even be good for your physical wellbeing.

If you want to volunteer, you can help neighbours with their housework or do tasks for them. If there is a social issue you care about – maybe the elderly, animals or the environment – you can find a local organization that supports the cause. Perhaps there is a peer support group you can join to help others with similar life experiences. You could even create a volunteer group in your school or local community.

Reach out

All Sorts Youth Project
www.allsortsyouth.org.uk

Supports and connects children and young people who are lesbian, gay, bisexual, trans or unsure of their sexual orientation and/or gender identity.

Crisis Text Line:
Text SHOUT
to 85258

To find free and confidential counselling, advice and information on all aspects of mental health, contact Youth Access at: www. youthaccess.org.uk

Teens in crisis
ticplus.org.uk
Text 07520 634063

Supporting children and teenagers with anxiety, depression and anger management, through face-to-face, or online counselling sessions.

Hopeline UK
Call: 0800 068 41 41
Text: 07786 209 697

Talk to crisis counsellors via phone or text.

For what to look for in a therapist or counsellor, and where to find the right one for you, go to Mind UK.

www.mind.org.uk

Glossary

attentional bias way you become more likely to notice things that you think about often. If you worry often, you might have an attentional bias to threat, or tend to notice possible danger

cisgender describes people who identify with the sex they were assigned at birth

cognitive behavioural therapy therapy that helps you identify and replace negative patterns of thinking and behaviour with positive responses

confidentiality protection by rules or promises to keep something private

emotional regulation being able to feel all your emotions but hold back some reactions when you need to

executive function mental skills that help you plan, focus, remember and do more than one thing at a time

feedback loop cause-and-effect system that makes a response stronger or weaker

hyperventilate breathe rapidly and deeply, leading to a loss of carbon dioxide in the blood

hysteria historically, a mental health condition similar to anxiety, usually applied to women

limbic system structures and areas of the nervous system that are associated with emotions, instincts and memory

maladaptive behaviour things some people do to ease anxiety that actually end up hurting them

microglial cells small cells found throughout the central nervous system

mindfulness focusing on the here and now; noticing your feelings and thoughts without judging them

phagocytosis process by which some cells change shape to surround something (like a bit of bacteria) and pull it inside the cell to "eat" it

plasticity ability to change or be moulded

prosocial behaviour things you do to help other people or your community

resilience ability to bounce back from hard times

selective advantage something that makes you better able to survive

trauma-informed care treatment for survivors of painful experiences that focuses on using your strengths to feel safe and in control

trigger something that sets off your anxiety or reminds you of a trauma

Find out more

Books

Feel Better: CBT Workbook for Teens: Essential Skills and Activities to Help You Manage Moods, Boost Self-Esteem and Conquer Anxiety, Rachel L Hutt (Althea Press, 2019)

Looking After Your Mental Health, Alice James and Louie Stowell (Usborne Publishing, 2018)

My Anxiety Handbook: Getting Back on Track, Bridie Gallagher, Phoebe McEwen and Sue Knowles (Jessica Kingsley Publishers, 2018)

Websites

www.anxietyuk.org.uk/
For more information about teenage anxiety, including case studies and how to find help and support, contact Anxiety UK.

www.mind.org.uk
Information for children, teenagers and parents about mental health and wellbeing and how to find support.

www.youngminds.org.uk/find-help/looking-after-yourself/take-time-out/
Strategies to encourage a positive mindset and tips for building and practising stress-busting techniques.

Comprehension questions

1

Your stress response helped your ancestors survive life-or-death events. Can you think of some major stressors (something that causes stress) for early humans? What are your main stressors? How do your stressors compare to those of early humans?

2

In the past, people were often called hysterical when they didn't accept social norms. How do you think society treats anxiety differently today?

3

Some people seem more resilient than others. List all of the factors you can think of that might make someone better able to deal with anxiety.

Source notes

p. 12, "Anxiety and depression rates . . ." Michael J. Bradley. *Crazy-Stressed*. New York: AMACOM, 2017, p. 6.

p. 21, "Neurons that fire . . ." Catherine M. Pittman and Elizabeth M. Karle. *Rewire Your Anxious Brain*. New Harbinger Publications, 2015, p. 30.

p. 22, "Feelings like disappointment . . ." Pema Chodron. *When Things Fall Apart*. Boston: Shambhala Publications, 2016, p. 14.

p. 23, "Anxiety disorders develop from . . ." Anxiety and Depression Association of America, "Anxiety and Depression," https://adaa.org/sites/default/files/Anxiety%20and%20Depression.pdf Accessed January 10, 2019.

p. 30, "Giftedness and ability can be . . ." Gail Saltz. *The Power of Different*. New York: Flatiron Books, 2017, p. 89.

p. 37, "It's common to have erroneous . . ." *Rewire Your Anxious Brain*, p. 53.

p. 39, "If the rise in anxiety and depression is linked . . ." Peter Gray, "The Decline of Play and Rise of Psychopathology in Children and Adolescents," *American Journal of Play* 3, no. 4 (Spring 2011): 454. http://www.journalofplay.org/issues/3/4/article/decline-play-and-rise -psychopathology-children-and-adolescents Accessed April 12, 2019.

p. 54, "What are we supposed to do with the evidence . . ." *The Power of Different*, p. 10.

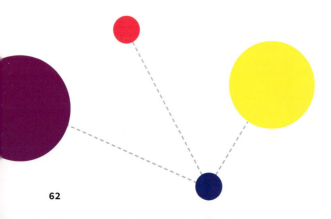

Select bibliography

American Psychological Association, "The Road to Resilience," https://www.apa.org/helpcenter/road-resilience Accessed January 10, 2019.

Anxiety and Depression Association of America, "Anxiety and Depression," https://adaa.org/sites/default/files/Anxiety%20and%20Depression.pdf Accessed January 10, 2019.

Bradley, Michael J. *Crazy-Stressed*. New York: AMACOM, 2017.

Brown University Counseling and Psychological Services, "Coping with Race-Related Stress," https://www.brown.edu/campus-life/support/counseling-and-psychological-services/index.php?q=coping-race-related-stress Accessed January 10, 2019.

Chodron, Pema. *When Things Fall Apart*. Boston: Shambhala Publications, 2016.

Cohodes, Emily M., and Dylan G. Gee, "Developmental Neurobiology of Anxiety Disorders," *Oxford Research Encyclopedias: Neuroscience*, December 2017. DOI: 10.1093/acrefore/9780190264086.013.129

Crocq, Marc-Antoine, "A History of Anxiety: From Hippocrates to DSM," *Dialogues in Clinical Neuroscience* 17, no. 3 (September 2015): 319–25. https://www.ncbi.nlm.nih.gov/pmc/articles/PMC4610616/ Accessed April 12, 2019.

Dartmouth Medical School, "Limbic System," https://www.dartmouth.edu/~rswenson/NeuroSci/chapter_9.html Accessed January 10, 2019.

De Becker, Gavin. *The Gift of Fear*. New York: Dell, 1999.

GLSEN, "Ruby Noboa to be Honored at Respect LA," October 12, 2018, https://www.glsen.org/article/glsen-proudly-announces-ruby-noboa-bronx-ny-be-honored-glsen-respect-awards-2018-student Accessed April 12, 2019.

Gray, Peter, "The Decline of Play and Rise of Psychopathology in Children and Adolescents," *American Journal of Play* 3, no. 4 (Spring 2011): 443–463. http://www.journalofplay.org/issues/3/4/article/decline-play-and-rise-psychopathology-children-and-adolescents

Greenberg, Melanie. *The Stress-Proof Brain*. Oakland: New Harbinger Publications, 2017.

Harvard Health Publishing, "Understanding the Stress Response," Harvard Medical School, May 1, 2018, https://www.health.harvard.edu/staying-healthy/understanding-the-stress-response Accessed April 12, 2019.

U.S. Department of Health and Human Services, "What Are the Five Major Types of Anxiety Disorders?" February 12, 2014, https://www.hhs.gov/answers/mental-health-and-substance-abuse/what-are-the-five-major-types-of-anxiety-disorders/index.html Accessed April 12, 2019.

Klemanski, David H., and Joshua E. Curtiss. *Don't Let Your Anxiety Run Your Life*. Oakland: New Harbinger Publications, 2016.

Martin, Elizabeth I., et al., "The Neurobiology of Anxiety Disorders: Brain Imaging, Genetics, and Psychoneuroendocrinology," *Psychiatric Clinics of North America* 32, no. 3 (September 2009): 549–575. DOI: 10.1016/j.psc.2009.05.004

McDonagh, Thomas, and Jon Patrick Hatcher. *101 Ways to Conquer Teen Anxiety*. Berkeley: Ulysses Press, 2016.

McEwen, Bruce S., "In Pursuit of Resilience: Stress, Epigenetics, and Brain Plasticity," *Annals of the New York Academy of Sciences* 1373, no. 1 (February 2016): 56–64. DOI: 10.1111/nyas.13020

Merikangas, Kathleen Ries, et al., "Service Utilization for Lifetime Mental Health Disorders in U.S. Adolescents," *Journal of the American Academy of Child and Adolescent Psychiatry* 50, no. 1 (January 2011): 32–45. DOI: 10.1016/j.jaac.2010.10.006

Our World in Data, https://ourworldindata.org/ Accessed January 10, 2019.

Pittman, Catherine M., and Elizabeth M. Karle. *Rewire Your Anxious Brain*. Oakland: New Harbinger Publications, 2015.

Primm, Annelle B., "College Students of Color: Overcoming Mental Health Challenges," *NAMI blog*, July 16, 2018. https://nami.org/Blogs/NAMI-Blog/July-2018/College-Students-of-Color-Overcoming-Mental-Healt Accessed April 12, 2019.

Saltz, Gail. *The Power of Different*. New York: Flatiron Books, 2017.

Tasca, Cecilia, et al., "Women and Hysteria in the History of Mental Health," *Clinical Practice & Epidemiology in Mental Health* 8 (October 2012): 110–119. DOI: 10.2174/1745017901208010110

Index

About the author

Melissa Mayer is a science writer and former science teacher who lives in Oregon, USA, with her wife, children and far too many animals – dogs, cats, rabbits and chickens. She's a bit of a geek and loves writing and talking about molecular biology and protein folding. She is a trained crisis counsellor who loves bonfires and hot springs.